Getting To Know...

Nature's Children

ZEBRAS

Bill Ivy

Grolier

Facts in Brief

Classification of Zebras

Class: *Mammalia* (mammals)

Order: *Perissodactyla* (odd-toed ungulates)

Family: *Equidae* (horse family)

Genus: *Equus*

Species: *Equus quagga (*Plains Zebra*)*
*Equus greyvi (*Grevy's Zebra*)*
*Equus zebra (*Mountain Zebra*)*

World distribution. Africa.

Habitat. Varies with species.

Distinctive physical characteristics. Black and white striped coat, the pattern of which varies with species.

Habits. Plains and Mountain zebras live in rigidly structured bands; the Grevy's Zebra tends to be solitary, though temporary groups may form.

Diet. Zebras eat only plants— mainly grasses, shrubs and herbs.

This series is approved and recommended by the Federation of Ontario Naturalists.

Canadian Cataloguing in Publication Data

Ivy, Bill, 1953-
Zebras/Bill Ivy. Rhinoceros/Merebeth Switzer

(Getting to know—nature's children)
Issued also in French under title: Les zèbres ; Les rhinocéros.
Includes indexes.
ISBN 0-7172-2605-0

1. Zebras—Juvenile literature.   2. Rhinoceros—Juvenile literature.
I. Switzer, Merebeth. Rhinoceros.   II. Title.   III. Title: Rhinoceros.   IV. Series.

QL737.U62I89 1989   j599.72'5   C89-093650-1

Have you ever wondered . . .

If you were asked to name a word that starts with the letter Z, what word would you pick? Chances are it would be zebra.

Few animals in the world are as well known as the zebra. In fact, it has even found its way into some common expressions. Can you think of one? Perhaps you have heard people say "a zebra can't change its stripes." They mean that you can't be something you are not. Another common expression, "a horse of a different color," was once used to describe the zebra. Today it means anything unique or different. That is certainly true of zebras. They are fascinating animals whose life story is filled with adventure, danger and fun.

The early Greeks called zebras "horse-tigers."

Horse

Zebra

What's the Difference?

How would you describe a zebra? A horse with stripes? Well, things are not always as black and white as they may seem! While horses and zebras are very similar in many ways, there are differences.

Zebras are not as tall as most horses, for one thing. And zebras have shorter, more erect manes and smaller, narrower hoofs. Their ears are larger than those of horses as well, and their tails are quite different. Zebras have long tails with short hair tufts at the tip, while a horse's tail is covered with long and flowing hair. Also, unlike horses, some zebras have a fold of skin, known as a dewlap, under their throats. And some zebras lack "chestnuts," those callous growths often found on a horse's inner leg.

Finally, there's one other big difference: unlike horses, which are mainly domesticated, zebras are wild and cannot be trained.

Zebra Relatives

It is easy to tell by looking that the zebra is a member of the horse family. The scientific name for this family is *Equidae* and it includes not only horses and zebras, but also donkeys and wild asses. Several of the zebra's relatives live in Asia and Africa. Let's take a look at some of them.

The ancestor of all domestic horses is the wild Przewalski's horse, which once ranged in central Asia but is now found only in zoos and reserves. Like the zebra, it has a mane that stands straight up. Wild asses are found in Africa and Asia. The African ass, the ancestor of the familiar domestic donkey, is very rare in the wild. There are several Asiatic wild asses. In general they are larger than the African species and more horse-like. The largest of all is the kiang, which can still be found in fairly large numbers in certain areas of Tibet.

The Przewalski's horse.

Curious Coat

There is certainly no mistaking a zebra with its black and white patterned coat. Take a look at the zebra on this page and try to solve this puzzle: is the zebra white with black stripes or black with white stripes? Most people think that zebras are white, since you can barely see the faint dark stripes on some animals. In some parts of Africa there are even zebras with spots instead of stripes on their hindquarters!

Surprisingly, not all zebras are just black and white. They may have brown, gray, yellow or buff-colored stripes. Often there are lighter bands, called shadow stripes, between the darker ones. But whatever the design, no two zebras are exactly alike. Their striped patterns are as individual as your fingerprints.

Bewildering Bands

The zebra's striped coat is certainly striking, but it is also useful. It helps the zebra hide from its enemies. A zebra's enemies see the world differently than we do. Just as we cannot distinguish color outside by moonlight (try it tonight, you'll see what I mean), many animals cannot see color at all, even in bright daylight. They see their world only in black and white and shades of gray. For this reason, the zebra's stripes make it less noticeable because they don't stick out against the background.

But that's not all. The zebra's striped coat also breaks up the animal's outline, making it very hard to see from far away. And when a herd of zebras group together, it is almost impossible to tell where one ends and another begins. This form of camouflage works very well!

How many zebras can you see in this picture?

Horse Sense

Zebras have razor-sharp senses—and a good thing too, because they must always be on the lookout for danger.

A zebra has excellent eyesight and can see much farther into the distance than we can. It can also focus up close and far away at the same time. How? The pupils of a zebra's eyes are not round like ours, but oblong. So when a zebra is feeding, it can focus on the grass with one part of its eye and look out for danger with the other part. (Try to do that yourself and you will instantly go cross-eyed!)

The zebra's other senses are also very important for its survival. Many times it will smell danger before actually seeing it, and its cup-shaped ears turn in all directions to funnel in sounds. In fact, zebras have such good hearing, it is almost impossible to sneak up on one!

The zebra's eyes are set well back on its head, enabling it to see all around.

Born to Run

The zebra is a superb runner. Its strong heart and lungs and its muscular legs let it bolt away with incredible speed. Zebras have been clocked at 100 kilometres (60 miles) per hour. That is as fast as a car speeding down a highway! While it cannot keep up this pace for long, a zebra can run as fast as a car driving down a city street for 25 kilometres (15 miles) or so.

Most of the time, however, a zebra's pace of life is not that hectic. Like a horse, it has three speeds, or gaits: walking, trotting and galloping. Usually it moves at an easy walk.

Whether it is moving fast or slowly, only one toe of each of the zebra's feet touches the ground. That's the fully developed middle toe, which is surrounded by a hard protective covering, or hoof.

Beating the Itch

Have you heard this joke:

Question: What's black and white and red
all over?

Answer: A sunburnt zebra, of course!

While the idea of a zebra with a sunburn is rather silly, too much sun *can* be harmful. The sun and hot winds can dry out a zebra's skin and make it itchy. In order to scratch itself, a zebra rubs against tree stumps, rocks and even its friends. To get at those hard to reach spots, it lies down and rolls on the ground. This feels good and covers the zebra with dirt and mud that help to protect it from the heat and wind.

Often a zebra is also bothered by tiny insects that burrow into its hide. This is where teamwork comes in handy. Zebras often nibble each other's backs to get rid of those itchy pests. This mutual grooming also acts as a soothing massage. After all, who doesn't like back rubs? Another solution is to take a bath—a dust bath, that is. Not the best way to keep clean perhaps, but it does help the zebra stay pest free.

Opposite page:
Once a good spot for a dust bath is found, several zebras may take turns using it.

Coarse Cuisine

Zebras never hunt. They feed only on plants. Their favorites are grasses, shrubs and herbs, but they will eat any available bulbs and fruits. Much of this food is very coarse. If we ate zebra food regularly, our teeth would quickly wear down. However, zebras have special teeth that are sunk deep into their jaws and grow throughout their lives. When one of a zebra's teeth wears down, just the right amount of tooth pushes up out of the jaw to replace what has worn away. Also, by chewing sideways, the zebra keeps the grinding edges of its teeth sharp.

Zebras spend as much as half of each day grazing. Most zebras must also drink daily. If there is not enough food or water available, they may travel up to 45 kilometres (30 miles) a day to satisfy their hunger and thirst.

Grazing in the grass.

On the Alert

A zebra's life is full of danger. Lions are its greatest enemy, although jackals, wild dogs and hyenas are also a threat. However, a zebra is not an easy prey because it is very cautious. Usually only the weak, sick or careless become the victims of a hungry predator.

Zebras know there is safety in numbers. When a herd is feeding or drinking, one zebra stands guard and warns the herd at the first sign of danger. At night, a male stallion stands guard. If an enemy attacks, the night watchman sounds the alarm. While the rest of the herd flees, he stays behind to face the attacker.

Zebras have another easy way of keeping watch. When two zebras stand side by side they face in opposite directions. That way they can keep alert for any surprise attacks.

Zebras are incredibly loyal. If a mare and her young are in trouble, a group of stallions will come to their rescue. If a member of the herd is injured or sick, the rest of the group may slow down to its pace. The elderly are also helped along and are even brought food.

Opposite page:
For added protection, zebras often gather around giraffes because they make such excellent watchtowers.

22

Meet the Family

If you want to see zebras in the wild, you will have to visit Africa. That is now their only home, although scientists believe they once lived in Europe.

There are three different species of zebras and they live in different parts of Africa. However, there is some overlap and, in certain areas, two types can be seen together.

The Plains Zebra is found in the savannah and grassland areas of the central and eastern flatlands. The Grevy's Zebra, sometimes called the desert zebra, lives in the low hill country. The Mountain Zebra inhabits rocky stretches of land in the southern part of Africa.

Plains Zebra
Grevy's Zebra
Mountain Zebra

The shaded areas on this map show where zebras live in Africa.

The Plains Zebra

The Plains Zebra (often called Burchell's Zebra) is still found in herds as large as 10 000. Most are fat-looking animals with short legs. Their stripe pattern varies from place to place: the farther south they live, the less prominent their stripes. All Plains Zebras have a black muzzle and a tail with a rather long tassel.

The Plains Zebra is the one you are most likely to get a chance to see for yourself—without going to Africa. It is the kind most often found in zoos.

The Plains Zebra has been described as rather dumpy. What do you think?

The Mountain Zebra

The Mountain Zebra is the smallest of all zebras. It has a brown muzzle, long tapered ears, a short tail tuft and a dewlap. Living together in small herds of about six animals, Mountain Zebras keep to themselves. However, if food is plentiful, they will group together in large numbers. Mountain Zebras can go for longer periods without water than their cousin, the Plains Zebra.

With its streamlined body, thin legs and narrow hoofs, the Mountain Zebra is well suited for its life in the hills. As you might expect, it is an excellent climber and can scale steep rocky cliffs with ease. Mountain Zebras are creatures of habit. They like to follow the same well-worn paths. These handsome animals are not very common, but fortunately they are protected in Africa's national parks.

Mountain Zebras.

The Grevy's Zebra

There is no mistaking the Grevy's Zebra. Standing over a metre and a half (5 feet) at the shoulder, it is the largest of all zebras and has longer, more rounded ears than the rest of its family. Narrow stripes that run very close together line most of its body from head to hoof. Only its belly is unmarked. A single stripe runs down its back and cuts its hindquarters in two. If you were to take away a Grevy's stripes, it would look more like an ass than a horse. In fact, its voice sounds rather like a donkey's bray.

Unlike other zebras, the Grevy's likes to be alone. Many people think it is the most beautiful member of the zebra family. What do you think?

The Grevy's Zebra is the most aggressive of all the zebras.

30

Rank and File

Generally speaking, zebras are sociable animals. They seem to enjoy each other's company—as long as no one steps out of line. Within each band there is one male and up to six females and their young, and each member has its own distinct ranking.

The stallion is the chief. Next in importance is the senior mare. When the band is on the move, she leads the way, followed by the second-ranking mare and so on down the line to the youngest zebras. Protecting the rear is the stallion, who chases away any predators. Each member of the herd is careful to keep in line. Should any of them try to promote themselves up a position or two, look out! Their superior will promptly chase them back where they belong.

Having seniority has definite advantages. After all, the first to arrive get first dibs at the drinking hole and the pick of the choicest grasses.

Opposite page:
Young zebras are well looked after by their family.

Making Tracks

When food or water become scarce, zebras must look for "greener pastures." Africa's dry season is particularly hard on them and sometimes they are forced to travel great distances to find a meal. However, even in the driest weather, grass can usually be found along rivers and waterholes. While migrating, some species gather together in large numbers. During this time, herds containing thousands of zebras can be seen crossing the plains.

The Plains Zebra travels the farthest, migrating hundreds of kilometres (miles) each year. The Grevy's Zebra also migrates, but does not cover such a large area. Even the Mountain Zebra seeks fresh new areas to graze on, although it stays within the boundaries of the African parks and reserves where it lives.

Searching for greener pastures.

Battling Stallions

While family groups of zebras are usually easy-going, fights between stallions frequently break out. Sometimes the stallions bicker over food or territory. Often a fight will start when one tries to steal another's mare, hoping to start a family of his own.

The match usually begins with a lot of foot stomping and pushing. The combatants flatten their ears back and snort at each other. If neither backs down, the battle heats up, and they bite, kick and neck wrestle until one of them decides he has had enough. The loser surrenders by lowering his head to show that he is beaten. Although these battles are often fierce, zebras do not fight to the death.

These zebras are not just horsing around!

Zebra Talk

When you meet a friend, how do you greet each other? With a friendly hello? When two zebras meet, they greet by sniffing each other. Zebras also use their voices to communicate. Each species has its own distinctive voice. They can growl, whine, snort or whistle. There are different calls for greeting or warning one another, showing contentment or expressing pain.

Zebras also use body language. How they move their ears, tail or mouth indicates what sort of mood they are in. However, to tell if a zebra is sleeping, you may have to check if its eyes are shut because an adult zebra can sleep standing up.

The call of the Damaraland Zebra (a Plains Zebra) sounds a little like a dog's bark.

Shaky Beginnings

Zebra babies may be born at any time of the year.

When the time comes for a female zebra to give birth, she leaves the herd and begins looking for a private place. An area where the grass is not too tall is perfect. Here she delivers her baby alone. The newborn zebra, or foal, has a soft shaggy coat of brown and white stripes which its mother immediately licks clean.

Shortly after birth the wide-eyed foal struggles to its feet. This takes a bit of practice and the determined little zebra may topple over a few times before finally learning to balance on its wobbly legs. The newborn huddles close to its mother and feeds on her milk. Within an hour, the foal will be strong enough to walk or even run.

This young Plains Zebra will be independent some time around its first birthday.

Horsing Around

Once the foal is steady on its feet, the mother rejoins the herd, and it may take a few days for the foal to learn to recognize her amid the other mares.

As their youngsters sleep on the ground, the females rest nearby. At the first sign of trouble, they wake the foals and run with them to safety. Within a few weeks the foals start grazing. However, they will continue to drink their mothers' milk for at least a year.

Like all children, foals love to play. Under the watchful eyes of their mothers, they frolic and chase each other. While this "horsing around" is fun, it is also important as it helps to develop the young ones' strength and sharpens their reflexes. The adults often join in the fun and play-fight with the foals. This helps to train the youngsters for any real fights they may have in the future.

Along with fun and games, the young zebras must also learn the rules of the herd. They learn to obey their superiors and accept their ranking order.

Stepping Out

Within one to three years the young zebras will leave their families to join other herds or start one of their own. In some species, the young males, called colts, group together in bachelor clubs for a few years until they are strong and smart enough to take over or form herds of their own.

Sadly, only half of the foals born will reach adulthood. However, those that do may live for ten to twenty-five years.

In the past, zebras were hunted for their beautiful coats, but fortunately many African countries have now formed wildlife parks where zebras can roam freely, protected by the law. There is no question that these beautiful animals are worth preserving.

Special Words

Camouflage   Colors and patterns that help an animal blend in with its surroundings.

Colt   A young male zebra.

Dewlap   A fold of loose skin hanging under the throat of some animals, including some zebras.

Foal   A baby zebra.

Gait   A particular way of walking and/or running.

Groom   Brush or clean hair or fur.

Hoofs   Hard nail-like growths that protect a zebra's feet.

Mare   A female zebra.

Migrate   To make regular journeys in search of food.

Predator   An animal that hunts other animals for food.

Reserve   An area where wildlife is protected by law.

Savannah   Flat grassland of tropical or subtropical regions.

Shadow stripes   Brownish bands found on some zebras between the dark stripes.

Stallion   A male zebra.

INDEX

Cover Photo: Boyd Norton

Photo Credits: Bill Ivy, pages 4, 8, 11, 15, 19, 31, 41; Hot Shots, pages 7, 38; Art Gryfe (Network Stock Photo File), page 12; J.P. Taylor, page 16; Boyd Norton, pages 20, 32, 34, 42; Harvey Medland (Network Stock Photo File), page 23; Metro Toronto Zoo, page 24; G.C. Kelley, page 27; B.E. Joseph (American Society of Mammologists), page 28; Four by Five Inc., page 37; E.R. Degginger, page 45.

Getting To Know...

Nature's Children

RHINOCEROS

Merebeth Switzer

Grolier

Facts in Brief

Classification of Rhinoceros

Class: *Mammalia* (mammals)

Order: *Perissodactyla* (odd-toed ungulates)

Family: *Rhinocerotidae* rhinoceros family

Genera: *Ceratotherium, Diceros, Dicerorhinus, Rhinoceros.*

Species: *Diceros bicornis* (Black Rhinoceros);

Ceratotherium simum (White Rhinoceros);

Dicerorhinus sumatrensis (Sumatran Rhinoceros);

Rhinoceros unicornis (Indian Rhinoceros);

Rhinoceros sondaicus (Javan Rhinoceros);

World distribution. Parts of Africa and Asia.

Habitat. Varies with species.

Distinctive physical characteristics. Rhinoceroses are large animals with thick skin, one or more horns in the middle of the head, and three-toed feet.

Habits. Vary with species.

Diet. Vegetation.

This series is approved and recommended by the Federation of Ontario Naturalists.

Canadian Cataloguing in Publication Data

Ivy, Bill, 1953-
   Zebras / Bill Ivy. Rhinoceros / Merebeth Switzer

(Getting to know—nature's children)
Issued also in French under title: Les zèbres ; Les rhinocéros.
Includes indexes.
ISBN 0-7172-2605-0

1. Zebras—Juvenile literature.   2. Rhinoceros—Juvenile literature.
I. Switzer, Merebeth. Rhinoceros.   II. Title.   III. Title: Rhinoceros.   IV. Series.

QL737.U62I89 1989   j599.72'5   C89-093650-1

Have you ever wondered . . .

It is a hot, dusty day on the African plain. Herds of zebras and antelopes gather around a waterhole, and a secretary bird struts along the edge of the pool. Several pairs of hippo eyes and hippo ears peek out of the water.

A snorting, puffing sound is heard from the nearby bushes and out into the clearing trots a huge White Rhinoceros. It wades noisily into the water, then SPLASH! Rolling around, the rhino covers itself with a thick coat of mud to keep it cool in the hot African sun.

But not all rhinos live in Africa or on hot dusty plains. If you'd like to find out more about these huge animals and how they live, keep reading.

A Big Little Baby

When a rhino baby is born, it looks very tiny compared to its mother. Nonetheless, it weighs up to twenty times as much as an average human baby—and it is not nearly as helpless. In fact, within hours it is up on its feet and taking its first unsteady steps.

By the time it is a couple of weeks old, the young rhino will be playing tag and wrestling with other babies, charging at its mom for fun or trying to sneak up on her from behind. Already it is learning skills that it will need when it's older.

Sticking close to mom.

Rhino Relatives

There are five types of rhinos. The largest one, the White Rhinoceros, lives on the plains of southern and northeastern Africa. Its closest relative, the Black Rhinoceros, also lives in Africa, anywhere from the dense rain forests to dry scrublands. The smallest of all the rhinos is the Sumatran Rhinoceros, and it's found in the southeast Asian countries of Sumatra, Malaya, Thailand and Burma. The Indian Rhinoceros lives on protected game reserves in Assam, West Bengal and Nepal, while the Javan Rhinoceros can only be found on a game reserve in Java in southeast Asia.

Scientists think rhinos' closest relatives are the elephant and the hippopotamus.

The Sumatran rhino is so timid that it is seldom seen.

Leave Me Alone!

Most rhinos like to live alone, except, of course, for a mom and her baby. Males usually remain completely on their own except when it's time to mate.

White rhinos, however, are a little more sociable. They live in groups of up to 18, including a male, several females and a number of babies, or calves. Indian rhinos will sometimes also live in small groups.

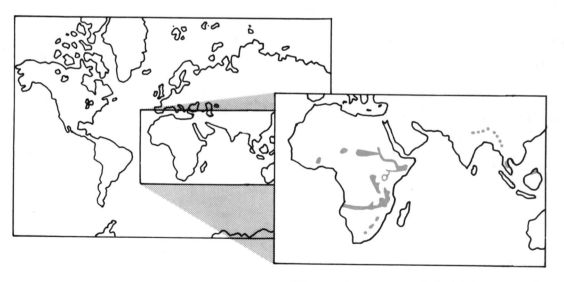

The colored areas on this map show where rhinoceroses live.

Home Sweet Home

Female rhinos live on territories ranging in size from 3 to 15 square kilometres (1.2 to 5.8 square miles) or even more when food or water is hard to find. One female's territory can overlap with another's and they don't usually defend the borders of their range. White rhino females often meet each other with nose-to-nose greetings, but Indian rhinos tend to be less friendly.

Males' territories are generally smaller than those of the females, up to about 4 square kilometres (1.5 square miles). However, most males mark the boundaries of their home range with their droppings and defend their territories fiercely against other males.

The Black rhino has a reputation for being bad tempered.

13

Big, Bigger, Biggest

You already know that the White rhino is the biggest rhino, but did you know that the only land animal that's bigger is the elephant? The White rhino is taller than most adult men and can weigh up to 3600 kilograms (8000 pounds). That's more than three small cars!

The Sumatran rhino is the smallest. It weighs only a little more than one small car and it probably isn't much taller than you. All the other rhinos are in between these two in height and weight. Females are usually the same size as the males or a little smaller.

Despite its size, the White rhino is peaceful and tends to run from trouble rather than charge.

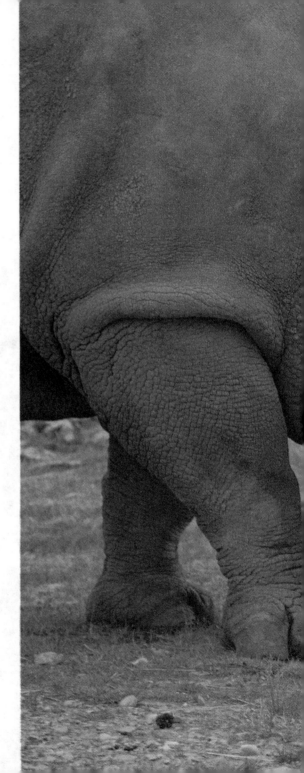

Horned Giants

All rhinos have at least one horn
—even calves are born with tiny
ones. In fact, the name
rhinoceros means "horn-nosed."
Indian and Javan rhinos have
only one horn, while both of the
African rhinos and the Sumatran
rhino have two. The two horns sit
in a row up the middle of the
rhino's snout, with the largest one
always in front.

The Black and White rhinos
have the biggest horns, and we do
mean BIG. The front horn of the
Black rhino is about as long as
your arm! Both these African
rhinos use their horns to defend
themselves.

*The rhino uses its horn to protect
itself or to help win the battle for
a mate.*

16

Hairy Horn

It's difficult to believe that something as hard as a rhino's horn is made of the same material as your hair, but it's true. The material is called keratin and is formed by the clumping together of hair-like fibers. Your fingernails and toenails are made of keratin too.

The rhino's horn may look like a cow's or sheep's, but unlike those animals' horns, which scientists call *true* horns, it has no bone in the middle.

Because a rhino's horn has no bony core, there's hardly any bleeding if it's broken off in a fight and soon a new horn begins to grow.

If you get this close to a rhino's horn, you're too close!

Sound Scoops and Super Sniffers

Rhinos are so short-sighted that they can't tell a person from a small tree at a distance of more than 30 metres (100 feet). And since the rhino's tiny eyes are over on the sides of its head, the rhino must turn its head to see anything in front of it.

But the rhino makes up for its poor eyesight with its excellent hearing and its superkeen sense of smell. A rhino's ears can swivel around so that they act like little "sound scoops" to pick up the slightest of sounds. And as for smell, the rhino's huge snout is filled with chambers that gather messages about the aromas drifting around.

A nose for trouble.

A Suit of Armor

Does the gray skin of this Indian rhino remind you of a suit of armor? Those large skin folds make it look like it's covered in overlapping plates that could almost be metal. These folds help scientists tell the difference between the types of rhinos. Both the Indian and Javan rhino have a skin fold at the base of the tail, but only the Javan rhino has a complete fold of skin like a collar around its neck.

The Sumatran rhino is easy to tell from its Asian cousins because it has long hairs scattered over its body. All other rhinos, including the African White and Black rhinos, lose their hair as they grow up, until they're left with just ear and tail tufts—and, of course, eyelashes! A rhino uses its tail to swish away flies.

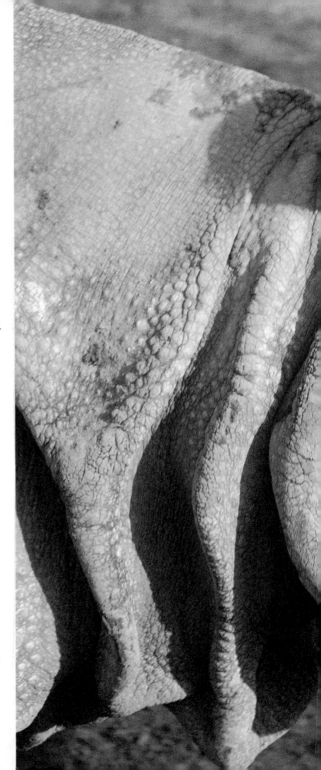

Meals and Mouths

Rhinos are plant eaters and they crunch down huge amounts of greens every day. Some rhinos graze on grass, while others browse on small shrubs, trees and leaves. Some feed on both and a few even eat fresh fruit. What a rhino eats depends on the shape of its mouth and lips.

White rhinos like to eat short grasses. Their wide, flat mouth and broad lips help them take big bites while feeding. These rhinos also have a hard ridge in their mouths to cut the grass stalks. The White rhino is the only one with a square snout, and some people think its name actually comes from the misinterpretation of a word meaning "wide" that described its broad mouth.

The Black rhino eats some grass but it feeds mostly on small shrubs and trees. Its tapered upper lip can grasp like a hand to tear twigs and leaves. The other rhinos also have skilled, rather pointy lips that can grasp branches and leaves and even pluck small fruit. The Indian rhino can also fold its upper lip to one side to make grazing on short grass easier.

Opposite page:
Given its size, it's no wonder a rhino eats huge amounts of food each day.

Grinders and Jabbers

You might think that with all those plants to eat, rhinos would need lots of teeth. Actually, they only need large molars to grind down the grasses and twigs. In fact, neither the Black nor the White rhino has front teeth at all!

The Asian rhinos do have front teeth, called incisors, but they use them mainly as weapons. Instead of relying on their horn to protect themselves, they attack their enemies by jabbing them with their lower front teeth.

"Look, kids, no cavities!"

Getting Around

Despite their short, thick legs, rhinos are surprisingly speedy. They can gallop as fast as 40 kilometres (25 miles) an hour, and a charging rhino can accelerate faster than a truck. And they can even change direction quickly.

All rhinos like to wallow in mudholes or shallow water, but they are also good swimmers. The Indian rhino is considered the champ—it can cross wide rivers and is a very good diver—and there have been reports of Sumatran rhinos swimming in the sea.

The rhino has a quite springy gait for such a heavy animal.

Club Tracks

It's easy to pick out a rhino's tracks from those of any other animal. All rhinos have three toes on each foot, a wide one in the middle with a smaller one to each side. As a result, a rhino's footprint looks like the ace of clubs from a deck of playing cards.

Each toe is tipped with a wide, blunt nail.

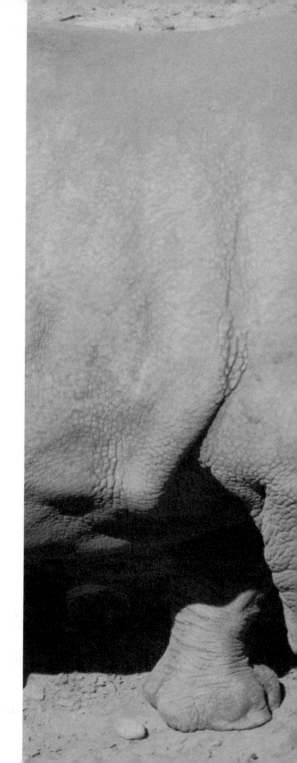

Happy Together

When you see rhinos in the wild, you'll rarely see them without little birds walking over them and picking at their skin. These small birds are oxpeckers and they've worked out a special relationship with rhinos and other animals.

In return for a free ride and all the insects they can eat, the oxpeckers keep the rhino healthy by removing pesky parasites. Along with cattle egrets, they also eat any insects the rhinos stir up as they walk.

Note the oxpeckers on these rhinos. They will even poke into their hosts' ears looking for a free meal.

Marvelous Mud

Rhinos spend a lot of time at waterholes. Indian rhinos like to lie in the water but African rhinos prefer to roll in the mud at the edge of the pool. They make giant mud puddles called wallows and roll in them until they're covered in a thick coat of mud.

Even though rhinos have thick skin, the outer layer is thin and has many blood vessels and nerves just below it. Insect bites and sunburn are very irritating to a rhino. A good coating of mud both keeps away biting flies and protects rhinos from the heat.

Nothing like a cooling coat of mud!

Daytime, Nighttime

Rhinos may be active at night or in the day, depending on where they live. Those that live on the hot, dry plains rest most of the day under a shady tree or in a cool mudhole. They only begin to feed in the late afternoon and often spend their nights grazing or playing and chasing each other at a waterhole.

Rhinos that live in cooler rain forests can be more active during the day, but even they will likely interrupt their wanderings now and then for a short nap.

Taking it easy.

Mating Time

Although rhinos tend to live alone, they do get together when it's time to mate. Often the female, or cow, will journey quite far in search of a male. As she travels through different males' territories, she gives off a scent that tells the males, called bulls, that she is ready to mate.

If more than one bull picks up her scent, there may be thunderous, head-bashing battles. Even the cow and bull may charge and battle with each other!

After mating, the bull sometimes remains with the female for a short time, but usually they separate and the female is left to care for her baby alone.

A pair of heavyweights.

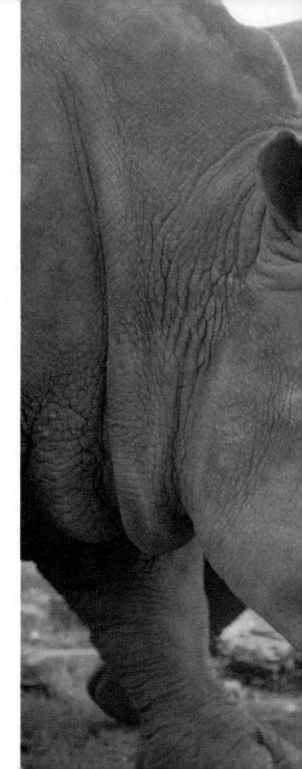

Welcome to the World

Fourteen to eighteen months after mating, the mother rhino gives birth. Almost always she has just one baby, but occasionally there are twins.

Just a couple of days after it is born, the baby is trotting along with its mother as she searches for food and water. The calf nurses from its mother and needs what would amount to about 100 glasses of milk each day! Within a few weeks of its birth, the baby is also eating grass or twigs.

The rhino is a very good mother.

Growing Up

A baby rhino stays close to its mom and nurses from her for about a year. She protects it from enemies such as lions, hyenas and crocodiles until it is big enough to protect itself. If there is a group of rhinos, they may form a defensive circle, backing together around any babies and facing outward. Few enemies are brave—or foolish—enough to tackle a wall of dangerous horns.

A calf will stay with its mom until it is about three years old, then it will find its own group or territory. By the time it's five to eight years old, it is ready to start its own family.

Following in mom's footsteps.

Rhino Alert

Rhinoceroses have been around for a very long time. Their ancestors, some of which had as many as five horns on their heads, roamed the earth millions of years ago. Today, five species remain, but the question is, for how long? Rhinos are among the rarest animals in the world. Scientists think there are less than 20 000 living wild, and they fear there are only 65 Javan rhinos left.

One reason rhinos are so endangered is that they are hunted for their horns, which some people mistakenly think can be ground and used as medicine.

There is hope for the rhinos, however. They are now protected by law, and reserves have been established. Their numbers are slowly increasing, and with some luck and enough care rhinos will be spending their days charging through forests or happily wallowing in mudholes for a long time to come.

Special Words

Bull   A male rhinoceros.

Calf   A young rhinoceros.

Cow   A female rhinoceros.

Incisors   Sharp teeth near the front of the mouth.

Keratin   The material that a rhino's horn is made of, as are fingernails and hair.

Mammal   Any warm-blooded animal that gives birth to live young and produces milk for them.

Mate   To come together to produce young. Either member of an animal pair is also the other's mate.

Molars   Large blunt teeth that are used for grinding.

Oxpeckers   Small African birds that feed on the parasites on the hides of rhinoceroses.

Reserve   An area where wildlife is protected by law.

Territory   An area that an animal or group of animals lives in, and usually defends from animals of the same kind.

Wallow   A mudpatch a rhinoceros makes to lie in.

INDEX

Cover Photo: Bill Ivy

Photo Credits: E.R. Degginger, pages 4, 12, 37, 42; Gerald & Buff Corsi, page 7; World Wildlife Federation, page 8; Keith Gunnar (The Stock Market Inc.), page 11; Bill Ivy, pages 15, 16, 19, 23, 26, 27, 33, 38, 41; Boyd Norton, page 20; Joseph A. DiChello, Jr., page 24; Jim Cronk, page 29; G.C. Kelley, page 30; Suzanne L. Murphy, page 34; W. Smyth, page 45.